MICROSOFT POWER BI

Learn The Basics in One Day

By

Dr Issa Ngoie

What is Power BI?

Power BI is a cloud based microsoft applications (tool) that allows users to connect data from different sources, Vizualize it, and share it.

> Power BI = - Cloud based
> - Connects data
> - Vizualize Data
> - Share data

Excel ← — Power BI → Quick Insight

Database ← — Power BI → Quick Insight

Introduction

Microsoft Power BI is a collection of software services, apps, and connectors that work together to turn your unrelated sources of data into coherent, visually immersive, and interactive insights. Whether your data is a simple Microsoft Excel workbook, or a collection of cloud-based and on-premises hybrid data warehouses, **Power BI** lets you easily connect to your data sources, visualize (or discover) what's important, and share that with anyone or everyone you want.

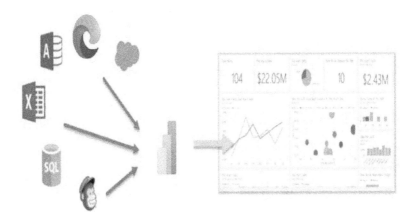

Power BI can be simple and fast, capable of creating quick insights from an Excel workbook or a local database. But **Power BI** is also robust and enterprise-grade, ready not only for extensive modeling and real-time analytics, but also for custom development. Therefore, it can be your personal report and visualization tool, but can also serve as the analytics and decision engine behind group projects, divisions, or entire corporations.

If you're a **beginner** with Power BI, this module will get you going. If you're a Power BI **veteran**, this book will tie concepts together and fill in the gaps.

Key terms

- ➢ Power BI
- ➢ Vizualization
- ➢ Local database

The parts of Power BI

Power BI consists of a Microsoft Windows desktop application called **Power BI Desktop**, an online

SaaS (*Software as a Service*) service called the **Power BI service**, and mobile Power BI **apps** that are available on any device, with native mobile BI apps for Windows, iOS, and Android.

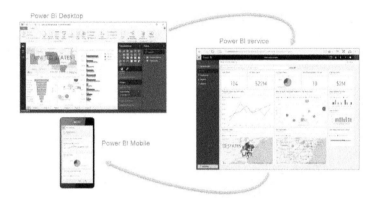

These three elements—**Desktop**, the **service**, and **Mobile** apps—are designed to let people create, share, and consume business insights in the way that serves them, or their role, most effectively.

Note:

> ➤ If you are a phone or tablette, you can use Power BI Apps.
> ➤ If you are a laptop or desktop locally, you can use Power BI Desktop.

> ➢ If you are using Power BI online, you can use Power BI services.

Exercise

Determine in which case you can use Power BI Desktop, Apps or Service.

1. A user wants to share his report online while analyzing it.
2. A user doesn't have any internet connectivity, but just a copy of Power BI
3. A User want to access Power BI using a tablette.

How Power BI matches your role

How you use Power BI might depend on your role on a project or a team. And other people, in other roles, might use Power BI differently, which is just fine.

For example, you might view reports and dashboards in the **Power BI service**, and that might be all you do with Power BI. But your number-crunching, business-report-creating coworker might make extensive use of **Power BI Desktop** (and publish Power BI Desktop reports to the Power BI service, which you then use to view them). And another coworker, in sales, might mainly use her Power BI phone app to monitor progress on her sales quotas and drill into new sales lead details.

You also might use each element of **Power BI** at different times, depending on what you're trying to achieve, or what your role is for a given project or effort.

Perhaps you view inventory and manufacturing progress in a real-time dashboard in the service, and also use **Power BI Desktop** to create reports for your own team about customer engagement statistics. How you use Power BI can depend on which feature or service of Power BI is the best tool for your situation. But each part of Power BI is available to you, which is why it's so flexible and compelling.

We discuss these three elements—**Desktop**, the **service**, and **Mobile** apps—in more detail later. In upcoming units and modules, we'll also create reports in Power BI Desktop, share them in the

Download Strategy	Link	Notes
Windows Store App	Windows Store	Will automatically stay updated
Download from web	Download .msi	Must manually update periodically

service, and eventually drill into them on our mobile device.

Download Power BI Desktop

You can download Power BI Desktop from the web or as an app from the Microsoft Store on the Windows tab.

Sign in to Power BI service

Before you can sign in to Power BI, you'll need an account. To get a free trial, go to app.powerbi.com and sign up with your email address.

The flow of work in Power BI

A common flow of work in Power BI begins in **Power BI Desktop**, where a report is created. That report is then published to the **Power BI service** and finally shared, so that users of **Power BI Mobile** apps can consume the information.

It doesn't always happen that way, and that's okay. But we'll use that flow to help you learn the different parts of Power BI and how they complement each other.

Okay, now that we have an overview of this module, what Power BI is, and its three main elements, let's take a look at what it's like to use **Power BI**.

Use Power BI

Now that we've introduced the basics of Microsoft Power BI, let's jump into some hands-on experiences and a guided tour.

The activities and analyses that you'll learn with Power BI generally follow a common flow. The **common flow** of activity looks like this:

1. Bring data into Power BI Desktop, and create a report.
2. Publish to the Power BI service, where you can create new visualizations or build dashboards.
3. Share dashboards with others, especially people who are on the go.
4. View and interact with shared dashboards and reports in Power BI Mobile apps.

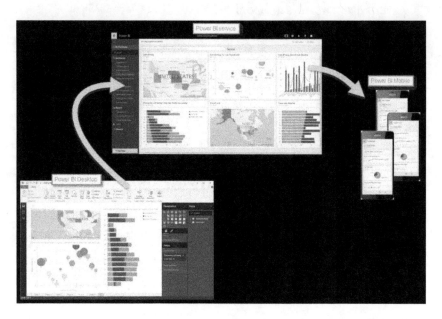

As mentioned earlier, you might spend all your time in the **Power BI service**, viewing visuals and reports that have been created by others. And that's fine. Someone else on your team might spend their time in **Power BI Desktop**, which is fine too. To help you understand the full continuum of Power BI and what it can do, we'll show you all of it. Then you can decide how to use it to your best advantage.

So, let's jump in and step through the experience. Your first order of business is to learn the basic building blocks of Power BI, which will provide a solid basis for turning data into cool reports and visuals.

Exercise

1. In which part of Power BI you can create a report?
2. In which part of Power BI you can bring data from the source in order to create a report?
3. List basics Power BI parts.
4. In which Power BI part a user can create a new visualization?
5. In which part of Power BI a user can interact with shared dashboard?

Building blocks of Power BI

In Microsoft Power BI, there are basic building blocks that make up the reports and dashboards consumed by end users. Think of it similarly to the basic construction materials that can be used to build homes or other structures.

Here are the basic building blocks in Power BI:

- **Reports** consist of **visualizations** and **semantic models** created with Power BI Desktop application.
- **Dashboards** consist of **tiles** from report visualizations created in the online Power BI service.

Visualizations

A **visualization** (or **visual**) is a visual representation of data, like a chart, a color-coded map, or other interesting things you can create to represent your data visually. Power BI has all sorts of visualization types, and more are coming all the time.

Visualizations can be simple, like a single number that represents something significant. Visuals can also be complex, like a gradient-colored map that shows voter sentiment about a certain social issue or concern. The goal of a visual is to present data in a way that provides context and insights, both of which would probably be difficult to discern from a raw table of numbers or text.

semantic models

A **semantic model** is a collection of data that Power BI uses to create its visualizations.

You can have a simple semantic model that's based on a single table from a Microsoft Excel workbook, similar to what's shown in the following image.

	B	C	D	E	F	G	H
C2132					2		
1	Year	Month	Month Name	Calendar Month	Births	Births Per Day	Births (Normalized)
2119	2004	1	January	1/1/2004	2,937	94.7	2842
2120	2004	2	February	2/1/2004	2,824	97.4	2921
2121	2004	3	March	3/1/2004	3,128	100.9	3027
2122	2004	4	April	4/1/2004	2,896	96.5	2896
2123	2004	5	May	5/1/2004	3,008	97.0	2911
2124	2004	6	June	6/1/2004	3,047	101.6	3047
2125	2004	7	July	7/1/2004	2,981	96.2	2885
2126	2004	8	August	8/1/2004	3,079	99.3	2980
2127	2004	9	September	9/1/2004	3,219	107.3	3219
2128	2004	10	October	10/1/2004	3,547	114.4	3433
2129	2004	11	November	11/1/2004	3,365	112.2	3365
2130	2004	12	December	12/1/2004	3,143	101.4	3042
2131	2005	1	January	1/1/2005	2,921	94.2	2827
2132	2005	2	February	2/1/2005	2,699	96.4	2892
2133	2005	3	March	3/1/2005	3,024	97.5	2926
2134	2005	4	April	4/1/2005	3,037	101.2	3037
2135	2005	5	May	5/1/2005	3,231	104.2	3127
2136	2005	6	June	6/1/2005	3,163	105.4	3163
2137	2005	7	July	7/1/2005	3,119	100.6	3018
2138	2005	8	August	8/1/2005	3,156	101.8	3054
2139	2005	9	September	9/1/2005	3,439	114.6	3439

semantic models can also be a combination of many different sources, which you can filter and combine to provide a unique collection of data (a semantic model) for use in Power BI.

For example, you can create a semantic model from three database fields, one website table, an Excel table, and online results of an email marketing campaign. That unique combination is still considered a single **semantic model**, even though it was pulled together from many different sources.

Filtering data before bringing it into Power BI lets you focus on the data that matters to you. For example, you can filter your contact database so that only customers who received emails from the marketing campaign are included in the semantic model. You can then create visuals based on that subset (the filtered collection) of customers who were included in the campaign. Filtering helps you focus your data—and your efforts.

You can create a Power BI report from almost any data, thanks to the many available **data connectors**, such as Excel, a Microsoft SQL Server database, Azure, Oracle, Facebook, Salesforce, and MailChimp.

After you have a semantic model, you can begin creating visualizations that show different portions of it in different ways, and gain insights based on what you see. That's where reports come in.

Reports

In Power BI, a **report** is a collection of visualizations on one or more pages. As with other reports you've seen or created, Power BI reports combine related data. The following image shows a **report** in Power BI Desktop—in this case, it's the second page in a five-page report.

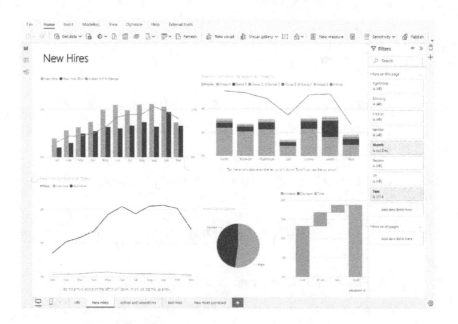

Reports let you create many visualizations, on multiple pages if necessary, and let you arrange those visualizations in whatever way best tells your story.

You might have a report about quarterly sales, product growth in a particular segment, or migration patterns of polar bears. Whatever your subject, reports let you gather and organize your visualizations onto one page (or more).

Dashboards

When you're ready to share a report, or a collection of visualizations, you can create a Power BI **dashboard**. Much like the dashboard in a car, a dashboard is a selected group of visuals that provide quick and important insight into the data or story you're trying to present.

Dashboards are limited to a single page, and allow users to follow a visual to the underlying report. Users interact with dashboards through the Power BI service or on a mobile device.

Tiles

In Power BI, a **tile** is a single visualization on a dashboard. It's the rectangular box that holds an individual visual. In the following image, you see one tile, which is also surrounded by other tiles.

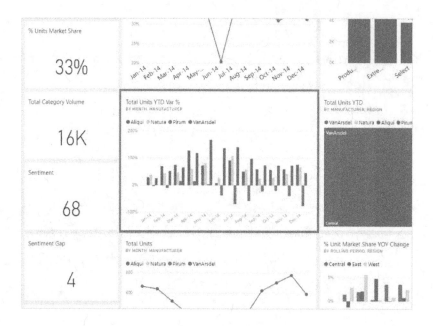

When you're *creating* a dashboard in Power BI, you can move or arrange tiles however you want. You can make them bigger, change their height or width, and snuggle them up to other tiles.

When you're *viewing*, or *consuming*, a dashboard or report—which means you're not the creator or owner, but the report or dashboard has been shared with you—you can interact with it, but you can't change the size of the tiles or their arrangement.

All together now

Let's review the building blocks of Power BI:

- Power BI Desktop lets you build semantic models and use visuals to make reports.
- The online Power BI service brings together reports, dashboards, and tools for easy distribution and management of your Power BI content.

Understanding the Power BI basics empowers you to create semantic models and design reports. Your reports don't have to be complex to be interesting and informative. Power BI offers easy ways to design reports from a single Excel sheet.

Power BI is also scalable, allowing you to create semantic models from various data sources, even incorporating custom code. The semantic model can then be used to design interactive reports and dashboards that emphasize crucial data for informed business decisions.

No matter how you use Power BI, it all starts with semantic models and visuals. These are the foundation for your reports that share insights and dashboards that present the most important data upfront.

Tour and use the Power BI service

The common flow of work in Microsoft Power BI is to create a report in Power BI Desktop, publish it to the Power BI service, and then distribute to consumers to view through the service or mobile app.

Power BI service allows you to create **apps** for easy distribution and clutter-free consumption.
An **app** is a way to group related reports and dashboards and distribute to the appropriate audience(s).

We go into more detail about apps (and the service) in upcoming modules, but let's walk through the experience to understand how apps benefit your organization.

Explore built-in sample reports

Easily explore built-in samples to get familiar using the Power BI service. Built-in samples are each a bundle of one or more dashboards, semantic models, and reports that you can use with the Power BI service.

From the Power BI service, open the *Learning center* from the left navigation pane. Pick one of the available built-in samples, which opens in Reading mode. Power BI then imports the sample and adds a new report and semantic model to your *My workspace*.

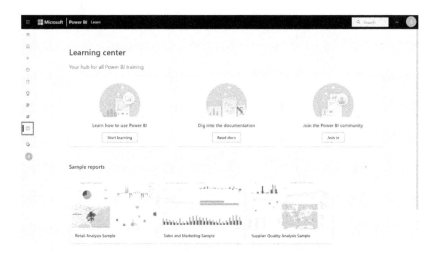

After you've chosen a sample report, you can see the direct report sharing experience for consumers. Take note of the Power BI service navigation pane and header, as shown in the following screenshot. You can see the report navigation and the filter pane, both of which are collapsible.

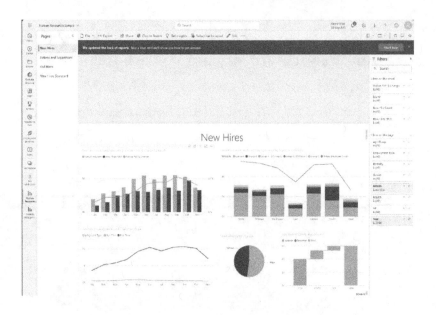

Explore template apps

Now that you understand how a report can be shared through Power BI service, let's look at the app experience. To replicate the experience, we're using the GitHub template app.

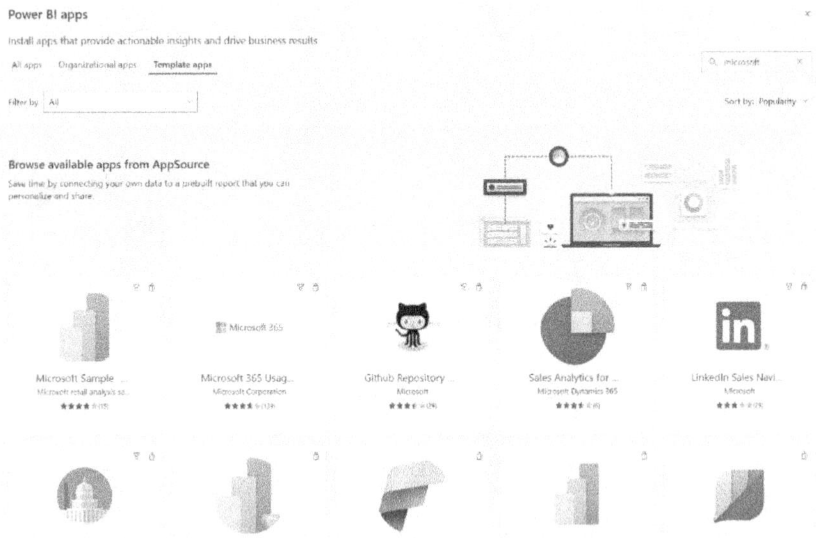

Tip

To access template apps, select the Apps icon from the left navigation pane > Get apps > Template apps.

In the following screenshot, you can see that the Power BI service left navigation pane and header that were visible with the direct report are gone. Also note the dashboard and a multi-page report in the app navigation pane. The app provides a cleaner look with only the relevant content. It's also customizable with app color and thumbnail. Apps also allow you to configure multiple audiences if you need to limit access to certain pages in a report, for instance.

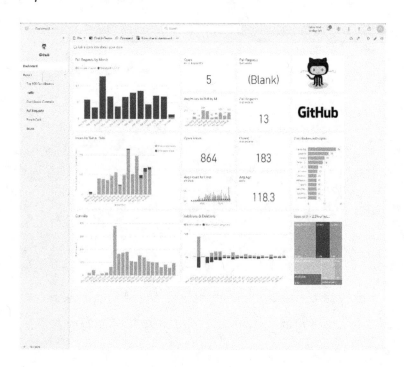

All of the visuals are interactive and interacting with one visual filters the others accordingly. For example, when you select on **mihart** in the donut chart on the **Top 100 Contributors** report, all other visuals only show related data for mihart.

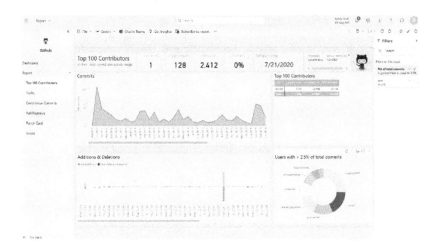

Refresh data in the Power BI service

Likely, your data changes regularly, so Power BI accounts allows on-demand and scheduled semantic model refreshes. From the app workspace, you manually refresh or schedule up to eight refreshes per day at minimum.

The **semantic models** tab is selected on the **Settings** page that appears. In the right pane, select the arrow next to **Scheduled refresh** to expand that section. The **Settings** dialog box appears on the canvas, letting you set the update settings that meet your needs.

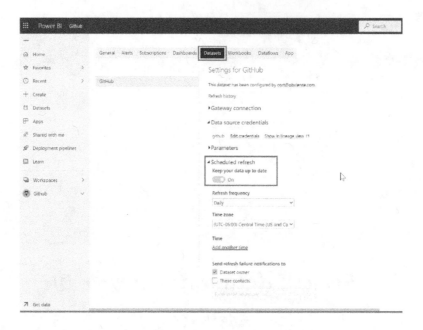

The Power BI service provides a simple and interactive user experience to take your data analytics to the next level.

Glossary for business users of the Power BI service

The Power BI service can introduce terminology that is unfamiliar or confusing. The glossary is a

great place to look up terminology—you might
want to bookmark it.

A

account
Use your work or school account to sign in to Power BI.
Administrators manage work or school accounts in
Microsoft Entra ID. Your level of access is determined by
the Power BI license associated with that account and
the capacity type where content is stored.
See *license* and *Premium.*

Admin portal
The location where Power BI admins manage users,
features, and settings for Power BI in their
organization.

 Note
Microsoft 365, Azure, and PowerApps use Admin
center.)

aggregates
When the values of multiple rows are grouped together
as input on criteria to form a single value of more
significant meaning or measurement. Only implicit
measures (see definition) can be aggregated.

aggregation
The reduction of rows in underlying data sources to fit
in a model. The result is an aggregate.

alert, alerts

A feature that notifies users of changes in the data based on limits they set. Alerts can be set on tiles pinned from report visuals. Users receive alerts on the service and on their mobile app.

annotate

To write lines, text, or stamps on a snapshot copy of a tile, report, or visual on the Power BI mobile app for iOS and Android devices.

app, apps

A bundle of dashboards, reports, and semantic models. It also refers to the mobile apps for consuming content, such as the Power BI app for iOS.

AppSource

Centralized online repository where you can browse and discover dashboards, reports, semantic models, and apps to download.

ArcGIS for Power BI

ArcGIS is a mapping and analytics platform created by the company Esri. The name of the visual included in the Power BI visuals library is called ArcGIS for Power BI.

Auto Insights

Auto Insights are now called *Quick Insights*.

BI

Business intelligence.

bookmark

A view of data captured in the Bookmarks pane of a report in Power BI Desktop or service. In Desktop, the bookmarks are saved in the *pbix* report file for sharing on the Power BI service.

PaaS

Platform as a service, for example, Power BI Embedded.

page

Reports have one or more pages. Each tab on the report canvas represents a page.

paginated reports

Paginated reports are designed to be printed or shared. They're called *paginated* because they're formatted to fit well on a page. They display all the data in a table, even if the table spans multiple pages. You can control their report page layout exactly. Power BI Report Builder is the standalone tool for authoring paginated reports.

pbiviz

The file extension for a Power BI custom visual.

pbix

The file extension for a Power BI Desktop file (letters pronounced individually as P-B-I-X).

permissions

What a user can and can't do in Power BI is based on permissions. As a *consumer* you don't have the same permissions as a *designer, administrator,* or *developer.*

phone report
The name for a Power BI report that's formatted for viewing on a phone.

phone view
The user interface in the Power BI service for laying out a phone report.

pin, unpin
The action a report *designer* takes when placing a visual, usually from a report, onto a dashboard.

Power BI, Power BI service, Power BI Desktop, Power BI mobile
Some of the Power BI offerings. *Power BI* is the general term. It's often used in place of a full product name, such as *Power BI service* and *Power BI mobile*, after the first mention of the full product name.

Power BI Desktop
Also referred to as *Desktop*. The free Windows application of Power BI you can install on your local computer that lets you connect to, transform, and visualize your data. Used by report designers and admins. **Power BI Embedded**
A product used by developers to embed Power BI dashboards and reports into their own apps, sites, and tools.

Power BI Premium
An add-on to the Power BI Pro license that enables organizations to predictably scale BI solutions through

the purchasing of reserved hardware in the Microsoft cloud. See *account* and *license*.

Power BI Pro

A monthly per-user license that provides the ability to build reports and dashboards, collaborate on shared data, keep data up-to-date automatically, audit and govern how data is accessed and used, and the ability to package content to distribute (Power BI apps).
See *account* and *license*.

Power BI Report Builder

It's a free, standalone Windows Desktop application used for authoring paginated reports. Used by report designers. Power BI Report Builder can be downloaded from the Power BI site.

Power BI Report Server

An on-premises report server with a web portal in which you display and manage reports and KPIs. It allows organizations to build distributed, hybrid BI systems (a mix of cloud and on-premises deployments).

Power BI service

An online SaaS (software as a service). **Premium workspace**

A workspace running in a capacity, signified to customers by a diamond icon.

www.ingramcontent.com/pod-product-compliance
Lightning Source LLC
La Vergne TN
LVHW060039070326
832903LV00072B/1383